DATE DUE

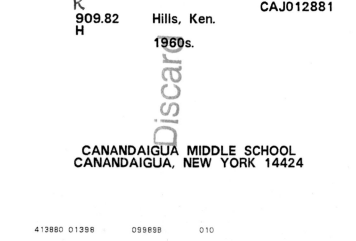

TAKE TEN YEARS

1960s

Library of Congress Cataloging-in-Publication Data

Hills, Ken.
    1960s / Ken Hills.
       p.   cm. — (Take ten years)
    Includes bibliographical references and index.
    Summary: Explores the decade of the 1960s worldwide, discussing such topics as the Bay of Pigs, President Kennedy's assassination, and the cultural revolution in China.
    ISBN 0-8114-3079-0
    1. History, Modern—20th century—Juvenile literature.
[1. History, Modern—20th century.]   I. Title.   II. Title: Nineteen sixties.   III. Series.
D842.5.H55   1992   92-30367
909.82′6—dc20   CIP
                                           AC

Typeset by Multifacit Graphics, Keyport, NJ
Printed in Spain by GRAFO, S.A., Bilbao
Bound in the United States by Lake Book, Melrose Park, IL
1 2 3 4 5 6 7 8 9 0 LB 97 96 95 94 93 92

Acknowledgments

Maps—Jillian Luff of Bitmap Graphics
Design—Neil Sayer
Editors—Caroline Sheldrick, Shirley Shalit

For permission to reproduce copyright material the author and publishers gratefully acknowledge the following:

Cover photographs—© Elliott Landy/Magnum; Popperfoto; UPI/Bettmann; Robert Harding Picture Library

page 4 — (from top) Popperfoto, Popperfoto, Popperfoto, UPI/Bettmann Archive/The Hulton Picture Company, AP/Wide World Photos; page 5 — (from top) Popperfoto, The Hulton Picture Company, Popperfoto, Popperfoto, NASA/Science Photo Library, Popperfoto; page 8 — Popperfoto; page 9 — Popperfoto; page 10 — Popperfoto; page 11 — Popperfoto; page 12 — (top) The Hulton Picture Company, (bottom) Novosti/Science Photo Library; page 13 — (top) The Vintage Magazine Co, (bottom) NASA/Science Photo Library; page 15 — UPI/Bettmann Newsphotos/The Hulton Picture Company; page 16 — (left) The Hulton Picture Company, (middle) Popperfoto, (right) © copyright 1991 Estate and Foundation of Andy Warhol/ARS N.Y./The Vintage Magazine Co; page 17 — UPI/Bettmann Newsphotos/The Hulton Picture Company;

page 18 — (top) Popperfoto, (bottom) UPI/Bettmann Newsphotos; page 19 — Popperfoto; page 20 — Popperfoto; page 21 — Popperfoto; page 22 — (top) Popperfoto, (bottom) UPI/Bettmann Newsphotos/The Hulton Picture Company; page 23 — UPI/Bettmann; page 24 — Popperfoto; page 25 — (left) Popperfoto, (right) UPI/Bettmann; page 26 — The Vintage Magazine Co; page 27 — The Hulton Picture Company; page 28 — (top) The Hulton Picture Company, (bottom) Popperfoto; page 29 — (top) UPI/Bettmann, (bottom) AP/Wide World Photos, (right) Popperfoto; page 30 — Popperfoto; page 32 — (top) Popperfoto, (bottom) AP/Wide World Photos; page 33 — (top) Popperfoto, (bottom) UPI/Bettmann, (right) Popperfoto; page 34 — Popperfoto; page 35 — (top) The Hulton Picture Company, (bottom) Popperfoto; page 36 — (top) The Hulton Picture Company, (bottom) Popperfoto; page 37 — (left) Michael Putland, Retna Pictures Ltd, (right) Popperfoto; page 38 — NASA/Science Photo Library; page 39 — Popperfoto; page 40 — Popperfoto; page 41 — Popperfoto; page 42 — Popperfoto; page 43 — Popperfoto; page 44 — (1) The Hulton Picture Company, (2,3) Popperfoto, (4) BFI Stills, Posters and Designs, (5,6) The Advertising Archives; page 45 — (1) The Hulton Picture Company, (2) The Advertising Archives, (3,4) Robert Harding Picture Library, (5,6) The Hulton Picture Company

TAKE TEN YEARS

1960s

KEN HILLS

RSVP

RAINTREE
STECK-VAUGHN
PUBLISHERS
The Steck-Vaughn Company

Austin, Texas

Contents

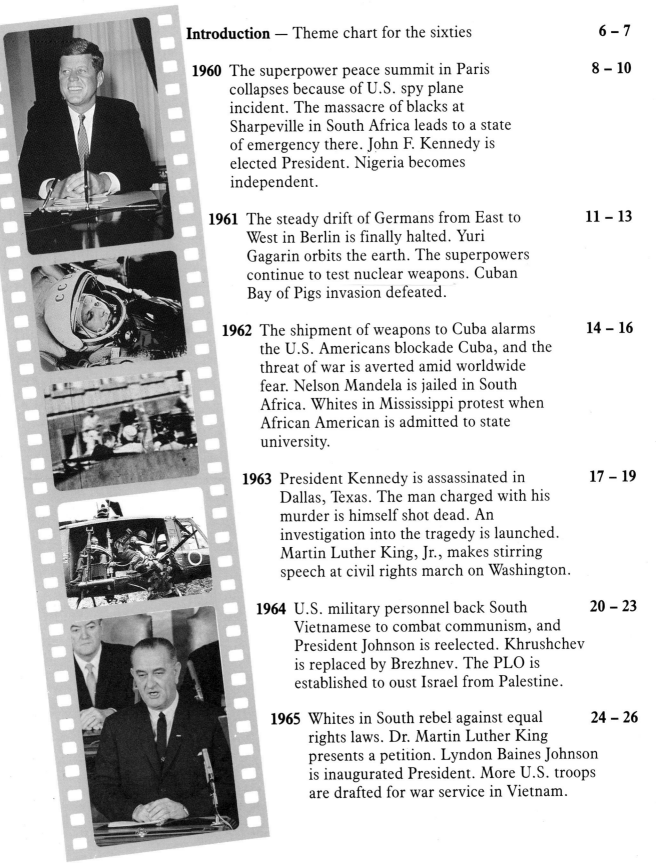

The pictures on page 4 show
John F. Kennedy
Yuri Gagarin
The shooting of Kennedy
U.S. troops in South Vietnam
President Johnson addressing Congress

The pictures on page 5 show
Mao Tse-tung
Francis Chichester's *Gipsy Moth IV*
Troops training in Biafra
Demonstration in Prague 1968
The footprint of Neil Armstrong's first step on the moon
A paper mini dress

Introduction

World affairs in the sixties were dominated by the enmity between the two superpowers, Soviet Russia and the United States of America. Between them, they held stocks of nuclear weapons capable of destroying the entire earth 20 times over. For a few terrifying days in October 1962, war between the two superstates over nuclear bases in Cuba seemed almost inevitable. But as the rest of the world looked on helplessly, the two sides paused to consider the fearful consequences of a nuclear conflict. Both agreed to compromise, and a war which might have ended life on earth was averted.

Wars were seldom out of the headlines in the sixties. As the decade wore on, America was sucked deeper and deeper into the Vietnam conflict. The age-old enmity between Israelis and Arabs boiled over into a violent six-day conflict which the Israelis won with astonishing ease. Other wars afflicted Nigeria and Cyprus.

The sixties were a decade of protest. In America, opposition to the Vietnam War, and the struggle for civil rights by African Americans, led to violent clashes. In South Africa, many died as the ruling whites cracked down on attempts by the non-whites to win equality and justice. In the Communist world, Soviet troops ruthlessly suppressed protest in Czechoslovakia. In Germany a wall was built across Berlin to prevent discontented citizens in the Communist East from leaving in search of greater freedom and prosperity in the West.

Numbers of young people in both America and Western Europe dropped out of normal life as a reaction to the violence of the times and turned to a way of life based on peace and love. They became the hippie generation and they influenced millions more with their ideas and fashions. Their feelings were expressed by the words and music of groups like the Beatles and individuals such as Bob Dylan and Joan Baez. Major events of the hippie movement were the outdoor rock music concerts. The most famous was the huge festival that took place in 1969 at Woodstock, New York.

The decade ended with the supreme triumph of science and technology, landing the first people on the moon, and returning them safely to earth.

YEARS	WORLD AFFAIRS
1960	U.S.A.-USSR summit meeting in Paris Congolese independence Nigerian independence
1961	East Germans flee to the West. East Germans close border at Berlin. U.S. and USSR test nuclear weapons.
1962	USSR ships missiles to Cuba. U.S.A. blockades Cuba. Threat of nuclear war averted.
1963	Assassination of J.F. Kennedy
1964	Palestine Liberation Organization founded Khrushchev replaced by Brezhnev as head of USSR Communist party. China tests atom bomb.
1965	Second Vatican Council ends.
1966	Cultural revolution in China India elects Indira Gandhi prime minister.
1967	Tension in Middle East Six-Day War gives Israel new territory. Colonels' junta seizes Greece.
1968	Czechoslovakia's attempts at liberty crushed.
1969	Czechoslovakian Jan Palach kills self to protest Soviet occupation.

WARS & REVOLTS	PEOPLE	EVENTS
Sharpeville massacre Revolt in Algeria	Gary Powers admits spying mission. J.F. Kennedy elected President. Verwoerd shot in South Africa.	U.S. spy plane shot down over USSR. Rome Olympic Games
British and Arab troops defend Kuwait. Bay of Pigs Cuban coup fails.	Yuri Gagarin orbits earth. Eichmann condemned to death.	J.F. Kennedy sworn in as President. Kennedy founds Peace Corps.

Race riots in Mississippi	John Glenn becomes the first
	   American in space.
	Marilyn Monroe dies.
	Nelson Mandela jailed.
	American painter Andy Warhol
	   exhibits Pop Art.
		Supreme Court bans school prayer.
		Richard Nixon defeated in California
		   governor campaign.

	Profumo scandal in London
	Pope John XXIII dies.
		Dr. Martin Luther King makes stirring
		   speech during civil rights march
		   on Washington.

U.S. sends troops to Vietnam.
Turks and Greeks accept cease-fire
   in Cyprus.
	Martin Luther King, Jr., wins Nobel
	   Peace Prize.
	Mandela jailed for life.
	Nehru dies.
	L.B. Johnson elected President.
		Tokyo Olympic Games
		Cassius Clay (Muhammad Ali) wins
		   heavyweight boxing title.
		Severe earthquake strikes Alaska.

Race riots in Alabama
Race riots in Watts
More U.S. troops sent to Vietnam.
	Sir Winston Churchill dies.
	Black leader Malcolm X killed.
		Civil rights march in Montgomery,
		   Alabama
		President Johnson signs Voting Rights
		   Act.

Major U.S. offensive in Vietnam
Australian troops go to Vietnam.
	Francis Chichester begins solo
	   around-the-world sail.
	Verwoerd murdered.
		Aberfan tragedy in Wales
		Flood in Florence, Italy, damages art
		   treasures.

Nigerian civil war
Vietnam war continued.
Six-Day War between Israel and
   Arab states
	Ronald Reagan becomes California
	   governor.
	Thurgood Marshall becomes first
	   black on Supreme Court.
		Three American astronauts killed.
		De Gaulle blocks Britain's entry to
		   Common Market.
		Supersonic aircraft Concorde unveiled.
		First heart transplant

Riots in U.S. after Dr. King's murder Nigerian war continues; Biafrans fight on despite defeat.	Martin Luther King murdered. Robert Kennedy murdered. Richard Nixon elected President.	Mexico Olympic Games U.S. astronauts orbit moon.
	Neil Armstrong and Edwin Aldrin walk on the moon. Dwight D. Eisenhower dies.	Yasser Arafat is new head of PLO.

1960

De Gaulle puts down Algerian revolt

Sharpeville massacre in South Africa

Feb. 1   De Gaulle puts down Algerian revolt
March 21   Sharpeville massacre in South Africa
May 5   Russians shoot down U.S. spy plane
May 17   Paris summit talks collapse
Nov. 9   J.F. Kennedy elected President

SUMMIT RAISES HOPES FOR PEACE

May 2, Moscow In two weeks' time the two superpower leaders, Premier Khrushchev of Soviet Russia and President Eisenhower of the United States, will meet in Paris. Their task is to try to end the distrust and enmity between their countries, called the Cold War. Both countries have nuclear weapons, and conflict between these nations seems to threaten to plunge the world into war.

RUSSIANS SHOOT DOWN U.S. PLANE

May 5, Moscow The Russians claim that the plane they shot down on May 1 was a U.S. spy plane flying over Soviet territory. The American State Department denies that the plane was spying. The U.S. announcement maintains that the plane was engaged in weather research, but was blown off course and accidentally strayed across the Soviet border. It carried cameras to photograph the clouds, says the State Department.

PILOT ADMITS HE WAS SPYING

May 10, Moscow The Soviet authorities have released pictures of the wreckage of the U.S. U-2 plane shot down last week. They have also produced the pilot, Gary Powers, who survived the crash unharmed. Powers has admitted that when he was shot down he was on a spying mission between Pakistan and Norway.

The accused spy pilot, Gary Powers, listens intently at his trial in Moscow.

PARIS PEACE TALKS COLLAPSE

May 17, Paris The talks here have broken up in angry confusion. The United States refuses to apologize for the spy flight. The Russians have chosen to make the most of America's refusal and are using it as an excuse for wrecking the peace talks. Khrushchev showed his contempt for President Eisenhower by stopping in the streets of Paris to hand out ballpoint pens to passing children when he should have been attending a meeting. It seems that the Cold War between the Communist East and the Capitalist West is colder than ever.

PROTESTERS DIE IN SOUTH AFRICA

Heavily armed police move among bodies of dead Africans outside the prison at Sharpeville.

March 21, Johannesburg Today 67 people were killed, and nearly 200 injured, at Sharpeville, an African township south of Johannesburg. Thousands of black Africans had gathered to protest against the hated pass laws, which require Africans to carry identity cards at all times. When stones were thrown, the police panicked and opened fire. More Africans have been gunned down at a similar demonstration. This one took place in Langa township near Cape Town.

STATE OF EMERGENCY DECLARED IN SOUTH AFRICA

March 30, Pretoria Unrest continues in South Africa. Black Africans are demanding the release of their leaders, imprisoned for opposing the apartheid laws, which keep black people in subjection to the whites. The police have been given powers to arrest and detain anyone whom they suspect may be a danger to the state.

AMERICA ELECTS YOUNGEST PRESIDENT

Nov. 9, Washington Only 120,000 votes separated the Democrat John F. Kennedy from his Republican opponent Richard Nixon in today's presidential election. JFK, as he is known, is 43 and due to become the youngest President ever to lead the United States.

THREAT OF CIVIL WAR IN ALGERIA

Jan. 24, Algiers Several thousand European settlers in Algeria have come out in revolt against the French government's plan to grant independence to the colony. The rebels are French, as are the troops stationed in Algeria. So far, the army commanders have refrained from ordering their men into action against their fellow countrymen.

ALGERIAN REVOLT CRUMBLES

Feb. 1, Paris The revolt that threatened to tear Algeria apart has collapsed. President de Gaulle appeared on television two days ago. He appealed to the French army in Algeria to remain loyal to him and to France. The de Gaulle magic worked. The troops have forced the rebels to take down their barricades and surrender.

BIRTH CONTROL PILL

Dec. 1, Washington Women in America and Britain will soon be able to buy a pill to prevent unwanted pregnancies. Scientists in the United States first discovered how to make the pill in 1951. Following trials on thousands of women, doctors are now confident that the contraceptive pill is safe. It will go on sale next month.

NEWS IN BRIEF . . .

RECORD ROME OLYMPICS

Sept. 4, Rome A record 5,337 competitors took part in the Rome Olympics, making them the biggest ever. The U.S. and the USSR topped the medal lists, but the star of the games was the Australian middle-distance runner Herb Elliott, who outclassed his rivals. He finished the 1,500 meters race three seconds clear of the rest of the field, in world-record time.

U.S. PILOT FOUND GUILTY

Aug. 19, Moscow A Soviet court has found Gary Powers guilty and sentenced him to ten years in prison. Powers was the pilot of the camera-carrying U.S. plane shot down over Soviet territory earlier this year. The Russians said the episode caused the failure of the Paris peace talks.

INDEPENDENCE FOR NIGERIA

Oct. 1, Lagos At midnight last night, Nigeria became independent. Nigeria was Britain's largest colony and with nearly 50 million people is Africa's most heavily populated country.

The Australian Herb Elliott wins the men's 1,500 m at the Rome Olympics.

GABLE DEAD AT 59

Nov. 16, Hollywood Clark Gable has died of a heart ailment at the age of 59. Gable had reigned as Hollywood's "king" in the 1930s. He starred in such notable movies as *It Happened One Night*, *Mutiny on the Bounty*, and *Gone with the Wind*. During World War II, Gable served as an aerial gunner in the Army Air Forces.

SOUTH AFRICAN PREMIER SHOT

April 9, Johannesburg Prime Minister Verwoerd has been shot and wounded. His attacker is a wealthy white farmer. The shooting follows last month's disturbances in which hundreds of black Africans were killed or wounded as they protested against the apartheid laws. Prime Minister Verwoerd will recover but white South Africans are shocked that this act of violence should have been carried out by a white man.

ARMY ACTS TO END CONGO CHAOS

Sept. 15, Leopoldville Army leader Colonel Joseph Mobutu has seized power in Belgium's former colony of the Congo. Parliament has been shut down and its leaders arrested. The Congo became independent on June 30 this year, under the leadership of Patrice Lumumba, and has been in a state of violent disorder ever since. There was an army rebellion, and both Belgian and United Nations forces were mobilized in an attempt to regain stability. Colonel Mobutu blames the politicians for the chaos in which the Congo finds itself. He intends to appoint a new government to restore order.

1961

EAST GERMANS FLEE TO WEST

July 31, Berlin East Germans at the rate of 30,000 a month are seeking a new life in the West. They make the crossing in Berlin, which is divided into sectors controlled by the Russians, the Americans, the British, and the French. There is a steady drain of skilled workers and professional people leaving the drab conditions in the East to seek a new life in prosperous West Germany. Not only is this a bad advertisement for communism, it also damages the economy of East Germany.

The East Germans build up the wall between East and West Berlin at a gate where there was only barbed wire. Families are being torn apart as the border is closed.

COMMUNISTS CLOSE BERLIN BORDER

Aug. 13, Berlin Early this morning, East German border guards closed the crossing points between East and West Berlin. Troops are laying down rolls of barbed wire along the entire frontier running through the city. All unauthorized travel across the border has been stopped.

A WALL DIVIDES EAST FROM WEST

Aug. 23, Berlin A wall has replaced the rolls of barbed wire across Berlin. Snaking from north to south, a concrete barrier 7 foot (2m) high now separates the two parts of the city. The wall is backed by anti-tank ditches in many places.

KENNEDY SWORN IN AS PRESIDENT

Jan. 20, Washington John F. Kennedy became the 35th President of the United States at an impressive ceremony today, here in the nation's capital. Millions watched on television as he called upon his fellow citizens to work for the good of America. ''. . . ask not what your country can do for you''; he said, ''ask what you can do for your country.''

The new President makes his inaugural speech.

Yuri Gagarin in *Vostok 1*, in which he made the first manned orbit of the earth.

RUSSIAN LAUNCHED INTO SPACE

April 12, Moscow The Russians have announced an extraordinary technological triumph. Earlier today, 27-year-old Major Yuri Gagarin landed safely after flying around the world in space. His historic flight in the spaceship *Vostok I* lasted 108 minutes. It is now up to America to equal and surpass the USSR in the race to put a human being into space.

SUPERPOWERS STEP UP NUCLEAR TESTING

Sept. 5, Moscow Over the last five days the Russians have exploded three nuclear bombs at their test range in Siberia. This action has broken an unofficial test ban and provoked America into resuming our own nuclear test program. The U.S. bombs will be set off deep under the Nevada desert to avoid spreading radioactive fallout.

FIASCO AT BAY OF PIGS

April 20, Havana, Cuba The attempt by anti-Communist Cubans to overthrow the government of Fidel Castro has ended in disaster. The invasion troops that landed at the Bay of Pigs three days ago have been either killed or captured. The Soviet government has accused America of aiding the invasion.

ARABS TO GUARD KUWAIT

Sept. 19, Kuwait City Troops from Saudi Arabia and other Arab states have arrived to take over the defense of Kuwait. They replace the British force that was rushed here last July to head off a threatened invasion by Kuwait's neighbor Iraq.

These British soldiers on guard in Kuwait will soon be replaced by a joint Arab force.

NEWS IN BRIEF . . .

KENNEDY FOUNDS PEACE CORPS

March 1, Washington Young men and women in America can now join an organization called the Peace Corps, which President John Kennedy unveiled today. Peace Corps volunteers will work on development projects in very poor countries.

MORE U.S. TROOPS FOR VIETNAM

Nov. 14, Washington Over the next two years, the number of U.S. troops serving in South Vietnam will rise from 1,000 to 16,000. Communist guerrillas from North Vietnam now control large areas in the South.

Ham and his nurse before the historic flight into space.

CHIMP IN SPACE

Jan. 31, Cape Canaveral, Florida American scientists have sent a chimpanzee named Ham 145 miles (240 km) into space. Ham was blasted off in a Mercury space capsule on an 18-minute flight as part of America's program to overtake Russia's lead in the space race.

EICHMANN TO DIE FOR MASS MURDER

Dec. 15, Jerusalem Ex-Nazi officer Adolf Eichmann has been condemned to death for his part in the killing of millions of Jews in World War II. Eichmann fled to Argentina at the end of the war and hid there under a false name. Israeli agents found him, arrested him, and brought him secretly to Israel.

1962

Oct. 1	U.S. race riots over black students
Oct. 16	Pictures reveal USSR missile sites on Cuba
Oct. 25	U.S. Cuban blockade proves effective
Oct. 28	Crisis averted in Cuba
Nov. 7	Nelson Mandela jailed.

THE CUBAN MISSILE CRISIS

Oct. 16, Washington The Soviet Union has been shipping weapons of war to Cuba ever since the Bay of Pigs invasion. Now the latest spy plane pictures show that the USSR is building rocket launch pads on Cuba. From there, nuclear missiles could be launched to hit the United States. President Kennedy and his advisors are considering most urgently what they should do to put an end to this new and deadly threat.

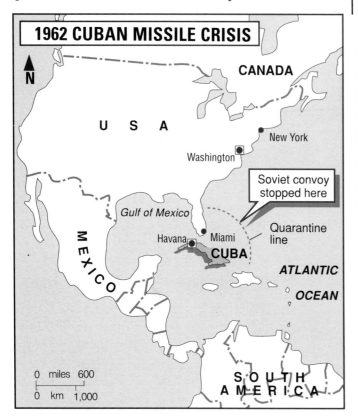

1962 CUBAN MISSILE CRISIS

N
CANADA
U S A
New York
Washington
Soviet convoy stopped here
Gulf of Mexico
Quarantine line
Havana   Miami
CUBA
ATLANTIC
OCEAN
MEXICO
0 miles 600
0 km 1,000
SOUTH AMERICA

The island of Cuba lies close to the United States. America imposed a ''quarantine line,'' or blockade, 500 miles off Cuba through which Soviet ships were not allowed to pass.

CUBAN CRISIS DEEPENS

Oct. 25, Washington Ships of the U.S. Navy have warned off a Russian convoy heading for Cuba. Twelve vessels thought to be carrying nuclear weapons turned around and sailed away before they could be boarded by the Americans. Meanwhile, work on the Cuban missile sites goes on. A nuclear war between the U.S. and the Soviet Union is now feared to be a very real possibility. Tension is very high as the world watches and waits.

ON THE VERGE OF WAR

Oct. 24, Washington ''I sat across from the President. This was the moment we had prepared for, which we hoped would never come. The danger and concern that we all felt hung like a cloud over us all . . . These few minutes were the time of greatest worry by the President. His hand went up to his face and covered his mouth and he closed his fist. His eyes were tense, almost gray, and we just stared at each other across the table. Was the world on the brink of a holocaust and had we done something wrong? . . . We had come to the edge of a final decision, and the President agreed. I felt we were on the edge of a precipice and it was as if there were no way off.''

(Robert Kennedy quoted in *Robert Kennedy and his times*, Arthur Schlesinger Jun., Andre Deutsch 1978)

THREAT OF NUCLEAR WAR LIFTED

Oct. 28, Washington The risk of a nuclear war over Cuba appears to have gone. The Americans and the Russians have both drawn back. The Soviets have undertaken to destroy their Cuban launch pads and ship all missiles on the island back to Russia. In return we have pledged not to attack Cuba and will lift the blockade immediately.

AFRICAN LEADER JAILED

Nov. 7, Pretoria, South Africa A court in Pretoria has sentenced Nelson Mandela to five years in jail. He was found guilty of planning a national strike and of encouraging violent rebellion by the non-white population against the white government of South Africa. Mandela's imprisonment may silence his voice for a while but it will make him a hero to the black people of his country.

In Alabama, firemen and police train hoses on 2,000 black demonstrators for civil rights. The crowd held a march and prayer meeting. Some 400 police and 250 highway patrolmen guarded the city.

LESSONS OF THE CRISIS

Oct. 29, Washington Russians and Americans have been badly shaken by the Cuban crisis. Both realize that a single unwise move might have pitched the whole world into nuclear war. We are trying now to work out better ways of talking to each other if dangerous disagreements arise in the future.

RACE RIOT AT A UNIVERSITY

Oct. 1, Oxford, Mississippi Only white students are allowed to study at universities in America's southern states. Blacks are not admitted. Yesterday James Meredith, a black man, arrived at the University of Mississippi and enrolled as a student. Thousands of angry whites stormed the college buildings and demanded that the authorities cancel Meredith's entry. A force of 750 federal marshals failed to restore order. Three people died and over 50 were injured in the fighting. Today President Kennedy sent in a larger group of marshals to escort Meredith to his classes. The whites continued to protest and a further 200 have been arrested. The rioting has spread.

NEWS IN BRIEF . . .

SERVICES FOR MRS. ROOSEVELT

Nov. 10, New York Former First Lady Eleanor Roosevelt was buried today beside her husband, Franklin D. Roosevelt. Mrs. Roosevelt has been greatly admired for her support of humanitarian causes. She was a delegate to the United Nations from 1945 to 1952, and in 1961.

FIRST AMERICAN IN SPACE

Feb. 20, Cape Canaveral, Florida America has put a man into space. John Glenn was picked up from the sea off Puerto Rico this afternoon at the end of a flight which had taken him three times around the earth. The space race between the U.S. and the USSR is gaining speed!

John Glenn preparing for the launch.

COURT BANS SCHOOL PRAYER

June 25, Washington The Supreme Court today ruled that official prayers in public schools violate the "establishment of religion" clause of the First Amendment. Official prayers in public schools are therefore unconstitutional.

COVENTRY'S CATHEDRAL RISES AGAIN

May 25, Coventry, England Twenty years ago last November, German bombers laid waste large areas of the city of Coventry and destroyed its cathedral. Today, Coventry's new cathedral was consecrated. It stands on the ruins of the old building and has been designed and decorated by some of Britain's finest architects and artists.

Interior view of Coventry Cathedral.

BRILLIANT BRAZIL KEEPS CUP

June 17, Santiago, Chile The Brazilians remain the leaders in world soccer. They beat the Czechs here today 3–1 and retain the World Cup they won four years ago.

NIXON DEFEATED AGAIN

Nov. 6, Los Angeles Richard Nixon, former U.S. Vice-President and 1960 Republican presidential candidate, was defeated today in his bid to become California's governor. "Pat" Brown remains governor. Nixon said he was quitting politics. He told reporters, "You won't have Nixon to kick around anymore."

MARILYN MONROE FOUND DEAD

Aug. 5, Hollywood The film actress Marilyn Monroe was found dead early today in her Hollywood home. An empty bottle of sleeping tablets lay nearby. Marilyn Monroe was enormously successful as an actress but a deeply troubled person in her private life. Her three marriages broke up and in June this year she was fired by her studio for repeatedly failing to arrive for work. It seems that her unhappiness has finally caused her to take her own life at 36.

ART CRITICS SQUABBLE

Nov., New York Is this rubbish or is this art? Andy Warhol's careful painting of a can of soup, now on view at a New York gallery, has art critics in a dither. Warhol is one of the new generation of American painters and sculptors working in an inventive new style known as Pop Art.

Big Campbell's Soup Can, 19¢ by Andy Warhol.

1963

DEATH OF A PRESIDENT

KENNEDY SHOT DEAD

Nov. 22, Dallas President Kennedy is dead. He was shot while riding in an open car through the streets of Dallas to a political meeting. His wife, Jackie, was at his side but escaped injury. John Connally, the governor of Texas, was traveling in the same car and is seriously wounded.

A Dallas policeman was shot shortly after the President was killed. An ex-marine named Oswald has been charged with the policeman's murder. Vice-President Lyndon B. Johnson has been sworn in as President of the United States. Kennedy's widow, shocked and dazed, stood at Johnson's shoulder as he took the oath.

OSWALD CHARGED WITH KENNEDY'S DEATH

Nov. 22, Dallas Lee Harvey Oswald has been charged with the murder of President Kennedy.

TV MILLIONS SEE OSWALD SHOT

Nov. 24, Dallas Lee Harvey Oswald, the man accused of killing America's President, himself lies dead. Oswald, under police guard, was being transferred to the county jail. A bystander stepped forward, rammed a revolver into Oswald's ribs, and pulled the trigger. Oswald died instantly. The entire episode was watched by TV viewers throughout North America.

President Kennedy in his motorcade cruises through Dallas minutes before the assassination.

In front of TV cameras, Jack Ruby shoots Lee Harvey Oswald.

MARCH ON WASHINGTON

Aug. 28, Washington Dr. Martin Luther King's stirring speech today was the high point of the huge "March on Washington." More than 200,000 Americans have come together in our nation's capital to protest racial inequality and to plead for justice and civil rights for all. Dr. King, an outstanding leader of the civil rights movement, is a firm believer in nonviolent protest. He gained the crowd's overwhelming approval with his address marked by the repeated words, "I have a dream." The Reverend Dr. King spoke of his hope that "the sons of former slaves and the sons of slaveowners" would one day be able to sit together as brothers.

THE WORLD MOURNS KENNEDY

Nov. 25, Washington Representatives from 93 nations have joined the American people in mourning the death of President Kennedy. Thousands of people, many in tears, lined Washington's hushed streets as the murdered President's body was taken to be buried in Arlington National Cemetery.

OSWALD'S MURDERER ACCUSED

Nov. 26, Dallas Jack Ruby, a local nightclub owner, has been accused of Oswald's murder. Mystery surrounds both that killing and the shooting of the President. If Oswald killed Kennedy, why did he do it? What made Ruby kill Oswald? Neither murderer seems to have had a clear motive.

JUDGE TO INVESTIGATE ASSASSINATION

Nov. 29, Washington President Lyndon B. Johnson has set up a commission to investigate the shooting of President John F. Kennedy. America's most respected judge, Chief Justice Earl Warren, is to head the inquiry.

Dr. Martin Luther King, Jr., is shown here greeting some of the thousands of participants in the 1963 civil rights demonstration in Washington.

NEWS IN BRIEF . . .

LOW LIFE IN HIGH PLACES

Aug. 7, London For the past two months British headlines have been dominated by a scandal. It involves a Cabinet minister, a Russian diplomat, a society doctor, a millionaire or two, assorted politicians, and a number of exceedingly pretty young girls. War Minister John Profumo, the central figure in the affair, has resigned. The scandal has rocked the government. An eminent judge has now been appointed to question those involved and to write a report on the whole miserable business.

John Profumo, former minister.

DEATH OF POPE JOHN

June 3, Rome Pope John XXIII, the best-loved pope of modern times, has died. Pope John was plain-spoken and warm-hearted. People felt he cared. He was a reforming pope, and in his brief four-year reign strove to bring the Christian churches of the world closer together.

SOVIET WOMAN IN SPACE

June 19, Moscow The Soviet Union, which began the space race, has achieved another historic first. On June 16, Russia launched a woman into orbit. Junior Lieutenant Valentina Tereshkova has become the first woman to leave the earth and orbit it. She returned today after making 45 complete circles around the earth in three days in her *Vostok VI* capsule. Parts of her flight were broadcast on television to the Soviet Union and to Eastern Europe. Soviet Premier Nikita Khrushchev spoke to her by radio. A male Soviet cosmonaut, orbiting at the same time in another space capsule, called Tereshkova "my space sister."

CANADA HAS NEW LEADER

April 22, Ottawa Lester B. Pearson, the leader of the Liberal party, has become Canada's prime minister. Pearson, a former diplomat and winner of the Nobel Peace Prize, spoke of his hope for an improved Canadian economy.

BEATLES MAY COME TO U.S.

Nov. 5, New York The wildly popular Beatles have just had their first No. 1 hit. It sold a million copies within three days of its release. It is rumored that the British rock and roll group will tour the U.S. next year. Frenzied crowds are expected to pack every performance here, just as in England.

The Beatles, seen relaxing backstage before their performance.

1964

WAR IN VIETNAM

COMMUNISTS GAIN IN SOUTHEAST ASIA

June 20, Washington The anxiety of the American government grows as the Communists strengthen their hold on Southeast Asia. Vietnam is most at risk. The country is divided in two. Red China and the Soviet Union support North Vietnam while South Vietnam is backed by the United States. Communist guerrillas, known as the Vietcong, trained and armed by the North Vietnamese, have overrun large areas of the South. Groups of specially-trained U.S. military personnel are serving alongside the South Vietnamese forces in a campaign to hunt them down. So far our troops and their allies have had little success. The Vietcong control most of the South outside the main cities.

A South Vietnamese woman abandons her burning village.

1964 VIETNAM

CHINA

N

Hanoi · Haiphong

NORTH
VIETNAM

Gulf
of
Tonkin

L A O S

THAILAND

· Hue

Bangkok

CAMBODIA

SOUTH
VIETNAM

SOUTH CHINA SEA

Phnom Penh

Saigon

| 0 | miles | 300 |
| 0 | kilometers | 500 |

South Vietnam is threatened by the
Communist North.

U.S. AIRCRAFT BOMB NORTH VIETNAM

Aug. 5, Gulf of Tonkin North Vietnamese torpedo
boats have fired on ships of the United States
Seventh Fleet patrolling the Gulf of Tonkin. United
States aircraft have hit back by bombing naval
bases on shore.

JOHNSON WINS ELECTION

Nov. 3, Washington Lyndon Johnson stays in the
White House. He beat his opponent Republican
Barry Goldwater in a landslide victory. Johnson
promises civil rights at home in America and
continued backing for the South Vietnamese.

PALESTINE ISSUE UNITES ARABS

May 31, Cairo Arab leaders meeting in Cairo have
set up an organization to unite the different groups
of Palestinian refugees. Many Arabs became
refugees when the state of Israel was founded after
the Arab-Israeli war of 1948. The new body is to be
called The Palestine Liberation Organization.
Saudi Arabia has promised to give the PLO the
money it will need to fight the Israelis. The Arabs
have named 1970 as the provisional date for the
war against Israel to liberate Palestine.

KHRUSHCHEV TOPPLED

Oct. 15, Moscow A plot hatched by his enemies in
the Kremlin has brought down the soviet leader
Nikita Khrushchev. Khrushchev, at 70, has been
replaced as party leader by Leonid Brezhnev and
as prime minister by Alexei Kosygin.

Nikita Khrushchev (left) on a visit to Sweden, with
King Gustav.

Lyndon Johnson during his presidential campaign.

TURKEY AND GREECE HALT CYPRUS WAR

Aug. 10, New York The Turks and the Greeks have accepted the United Nations terms for a cease-fire in Cyprus. This agreement ends, for the time being, the fighting between the Greek and Turkish communities who both live on the island. The peace is unlikely to last, for the hatred between Greeks and Turks is as bitter as ever. Furthermore, the Greeks disagree among themselves. Many regard their leader, Archbishop Makarios, as a traitor for agreeing to the UN plan. There have already been several attempts to kill him.

The Cypriot president, Archbishop Makarios, inspects Greek Cypriot troops in Nicosia.

NEWS IN BRIEF . . .

CLAY WINS WORLD HEAVYWEIGHT TITLE

Feb. 25, Miami Beach, Fla. Cassius Clay has proved his critics wrong by winning tonight's world title bout against Sonny Liston in seven rounds. Clay boasts ''I am the greatest!'' and he is without doubt a superb boxer. He has other talents. He has a record on the pop charts and can hold his own with any talk-show host. In the ring or out of it, Cassius Clay is a vibrant and memorable personality.

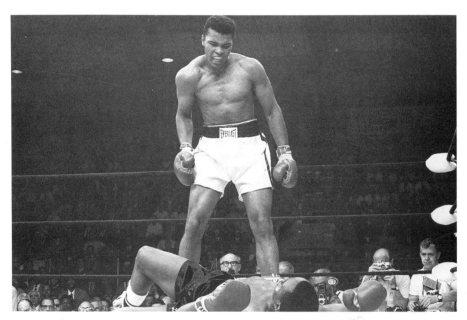

Cassius Clay stands over the fallen Sonny Liston during the first minute of their fight.

EARTHQUAKE HITS ALASKA

March 28, Anchorage The strongest earthquake ever to strike North America hit 80 miles east of this city yesterday. It was followed by a 50-foot-high wave. There has been extensive damage, and it is estimated that the death toll will reach 130.

DEATH OF INDIA'S NEHRU

May 28, New Delhi Jawaharlal Nehru, India's prime minister, died suddenly yesterday of a heart attack. Mr. Nehru will be mourned by millions of Indians and by his admirers throughout the world. He was a leader in the struggle for India's freedom and has guided the country since independence was achieved in 1947. World leaders are now gathering in New Delhi for the dead premier's cremation, which will take place tomorrow. His ashes will be cast into the water where the Ganges and Jumna rivers meet.

THE TOKYO OLYMPICS

Oct. 24, Tokyo The world record for the pole vault was broken 17 times between the Rome Olympics and this year's Tokyo games. The last two times it was by American Fred Hansen. This week in Tokyo, in a competition that lasted almost 9 hours, Hansen, of Cuero, Texas, set a record of 16 feet, 8 3/4 inches. Hansen said he won because he was thinking of what he could do for his country, not for himself.

Soviet athletes top the winners' list at the Tokyo Olympics with 96 medals. The United States follows with 90. Japan did well in gymnastics and wrestling.

LIFE SENTENCE FOR MANDELA

June 14, Pretoria Nelson Mandela has been sentenced to life imprisonment for sabotage and for plotting against the white government of South Africa.

MARTIN LUTHER KING HONORED

Oct. 24, Oslo The Nobel Peace Prize for 1964 has gone to Dr. Martin Luther King, leader of the equal rights campaign for black people in America.

CHINA'S ATOM BOMB

Oct. 16, Peking The Chinese exploded their first atom bomb today at a test site in Sinkiang. The United States, the USSR, Britain, and France have the bomb. China now becomes the fifth member of the world nuclear club. The Chinese claim that they built the bomb to protect themselves against the United States. They say the Americans want to plunge the world into nuclear war.

America's Bob Hayes (center) was the gold-medal winner of the 1964 Tokyo Olympics 100-meter dash.

1965

THE CIVIL RIGHTS BATTLE
VIOLENCE IN ALABAMA

March 10, Selma, Alabama The white population of this small town in America's Deep South are up in arms. They are protesting because regulations that prevented black people from voting in elections have been made illegal. Two days ago, Selma police armed with clubs and whips broke up a protest march of local blacks. The marchers were not violent, and there was no excuse for the police to attack them.

Today, there is news of a white clergyman beaten almost to death by other whites as he left a church used by black people. Other unprovoked violent attacks by whites on black people, and on whites who support them, are reported from several places in the South.

State troopers attack Negro John Lewis at Selma, Alabama. Mr. Lewis was later admitted to a hospital.

CIVIL RIGHTS MARCH

March 25, Montgomery, Alabama A crowd of 25,000 demonstrators massed today in Alabama's capital to deliver a civil rights petition to state governor Wallace. The presentation came at the end of a 50-mile (80 km) march from Selma, headed by civil rights leader Dr. Martin Luther King. Several well-known sympathizers were there to greet the marchers: singers Joan Baez and Harry Belafonte, entertainer Sammy Davis, Jr., novelist James Baldwin, and conductor Leonard Bernstein. Critics of Dr. King say that he is turning the civil rights movement into a branch of show business.

Dr. Martin Luther King arrives at the Alabama State Capitol to present his petition.

VICTORY FOR CIVIL RIGHTS

Aug. 6, Washington The Voting Rights Act is now law. The act, signed by President Johnson in the presence of civil rights leaders, will give the vote to hundreds of thousands of black people in America's southern states. The long supremacy of the whites in the South may be about to end.

RACE HATRED EXPLODES

Aug. 17, Watts, Los Angeles Five days of savage rioting have devastated this drab suburb of Los Angeles. Police brutality against local blacks brought out crowds of protesters who turned on the police, attacked whites, and destroyed property. The orgy of burning, looting, and violence ended only after 18,000 National Guardsmen had been brought in to suppress it. A commission is to be set up to inquire into the causes of the riots. People who know Watts say that the misery and resentment of poverty and high unemployment caused the recent outburst.

JOHNSON INAUGURATED

Jan. 20, Washington Lyndon Baines Johnson became President upon the death of President Kennedy in 1963. Today he was sworn in to begin his first full term in office. Johnson was elected in a landslide victory over Republican candidate Barry Goldwater. The oath was administered by Chief Justice Earl Warren in a traditional ceremony at the East Front of the Capitol. Hubert H. Humphrey, a former senator from Minnesota, will serve as Johnson's Vice-President.

Lady Bird Johnson watches her husband, Lyndon B. Johnson, as he takes the oath of office.

VATICAN COUNCIL ENDS

Dec. 8, Rome Today Pope Paul VI brought to an end the fourth and final session of the Second Vatican Council. This meeting of Roman Catholic Church leaders from all over the world has been one of the most important religious events of the century. Opened by Pope John XXIII on October 11, 1962, it issued a series of papers intended to renew and modernize the Church.

U.S. TROOPS POUR INTO VIETNAM

Dec. 31, Washington Back in July, President Johnson pledged that in Vietnam the Americans would not surrender or retreat. Increasing numbers of young Americans are being drafted into the war in Indo-China to back his promise. U.S. troops serving in Vietnam now number 184,000. The monthly number has risen from 17,000 to 35,000 in order to support the war effort.

NEWS IN BRIEF . . .

WORLD'S FAREWELL TO CHURCHILL

Jan. 30, London Winston Churchill died six days ago. He was by turns soldier, war reporter, novelist, historian, painter, politician, and world statesman. He has been honored in a funeral fit for a king. Leading figures of 110 nations came to London to pay their respects. After the service in St. Paul's Cathedral, Churchill's body was taken for burial in the churchyard at Bladon in Oxfordshire. It is close by the palace of Blenheim where he was born 90 years ago.

Sailors flank Churchill's coffin in the huge funeral procession.

SHORT SKIRTS RAISE PROBLEMS

Sept., London Paris invented the miniskirt, but it is London dress designer Mary Quant who has made it popular. Rising hemlines are now causing problems, particularly at British schools. To their pupils' fury, many schools insist that a school uniform skirt should be long enough to touch the ground when the girl kneels down. On the other hand, boys are in trouble if their hair is too long. Hair "above the collar" is the general regulation.

UFO SIGHTINGS

Aug. 2, Topeka, Kansas Last night officials in this state and in Oklahoma, Texas, and New Mexico, received many reports of unidentified flying objects. The "UFO's" were also seen by highway patrol officers and tracked on radar by Tinker Air Force Base. However, authorities say that viewers saw only the planet Jupiter or various stars.

BLACKOUT HITS 9 STATES

Nov. 10, Albany, N.Y. Last night 9 northeastern states went dark in the nation's worst power failure.

MALCOLM X KILLED

Feb. 21, New York Negro leader Malcolm X was shot dead today. Three men, including two members of the Black Muslims, were arrested for the crime.

1966

CHAIRMAN MAO'S NEW REVOLUTION

Oct. 30, Peking The chairman of the Chinese Communist party, Mao Tsc-tung, is using the young people of China to bring about a "cultural revolution." He believes that violent changes are necessary to make China into an ideal Communist state. Urged on by Mao in his speeches and writings, millions of students have left their studies. They dress in army uniforms and wear red armbands. Mao calls them his Red Guards.

RED GUARDS TERRORIZE CHINA

Nov. 19, Peking China is in turmoil. Mobs of teenage Red Guards have attacked and, in some cases, killed their teachers. People who seem to be too well-off to be true Communists are taken from their homes and forced to work on farms or in factories. Ancient temples have been destroyed and precious works of art smashed. Chairman Mao teaches that such valuable things are harmful or set a bad example in modern China.

The Chinese cultural revolution is felt even in Britain. These Chinese demonstrators are in London.

MAJOR OFFENSIVE IN VIETNAM

Jan. 9, Saigon The Americans are taking over this jungle war. Until now, U.S. troops have only gone into action at the request of the South Vietnamese. Yesterday, in the heaviest fighting since war started, the U.S. Command ignored our allies and made an all-American attack on the Vietcong.

NEHRU'S DAUGHTER TO LEAD INDIA

Jan. 19, New Delhi Large crowds gathered outside Parliament House to cheer Indira Gandhi when it became known that she had been elected to lead India's government. Mrs. Gandhi is the daughter of Jawaharlal Nehru, the first prime minister of independent India. In her first speech, the new prime minister promised to follow her father's policy of peace toward all nations.

GROWING U.S. FORCE IN VIETNAM

Dec. 31, Saigon Total American strength in South Vietnam has risen to 385,000 troops.

Mrs. Gandhi and the Indian high commissioner in London, Mr. Mehta.

NEWS IN BRIEF . . .

AUSSIES JOIN IN VIETNAM WAR

April 20, Saigon The Australian government is sending troops to Vietnam to join the Americans in the fight against the Communists. The first group flew into Vietnam this morning.

SOLO SAIL AROUND WORLD

Aug. 27, Plymouth, England Francis Chichester, 65-year-old adventurer, left here today on a journey around the world. He is sailing alone in his 53-foot sailboat *Gipsy Moth IV*. Chichester plans to put into port only once on his 30,000-mile (49,000-km) trip. He hopes to reach harbor in Sydney, Australia, in 100 days. An experienced sailor, Chichester in 1960 won the first single-handed transatlantic sailing race.

Luci Johnson Nugent and her bridegroom cut their wedding cake as President and Mrs. Johnson look on.

ASSASSIN KNIFES PREMIER

Sept. 6, Cape Town, South Africa Dr. Hendrik Verwoerd, prime minister of South Africa, has been murdered in the House of Assembly. He was stabbed four times and died instantly. Other government ministers over-powered the assassin. The killer is a white man named Dimitri Tsafendas. He seems to have borne a grudge against the prime minister. Fellow workers say he blamed the government for doing too little to help poor whites in South Africa.

Dr. Hendrik Verwoerd, South African premier

PRESIDENT'S DAUGHTER MARRIES

Aug. 6, Washington President Johnson's daughter Luci was married today to Patrick J. Nugent. The ceremony took place in the Shrine of the Immaculate Conception in the capital. Mrs. Nugent is the first daughter of a President to marry while her father was in the White House since 1914.

FLOOD DAMAGES ART

Nov. 8, Florence, Italy Three days ago, a violent storm caused the Arno River to overflow its banks. The resulting flood has damaged or destroyed many of the world's greatest art treasures in this city's galleries, churches, libraries, and museums. It is hoped that some of the damage to art and books can be repaired.

WELSH SCHOOL ENGULFED

Oct. 27, Aberfan, Wales Six days ago, over 130 people died in this small Welsh village; 116 of them were children. They were killed as a huge pile of coal overlooking the village slid down the hillside and swallowed up the school. The pile also included thousands of tons of wet mud and rock. There were scenes of heartrending grief as 82 of the victims were buried today. The government has ordered a high-level inquiry into the cause of the disaster.

Volunteers try to save valuable flood-damaged books.

1967

MIDDLE EAST TENSION GROWS

April 30, Damascus, Syria The Middle East is edging toward conflict. Palestinian Al-Fatah guerrillas make daily raids into Israel from bases in Jordan and Syria. Syrian guns on the Golan Heights regularly shell Israeli settlements on the plains below. Israeli aircraft have struck back at the Syrian gun positions. Across Israel's southern border, President Gamal Abdel Nasser of Egypt declares he is preparing his country for war.

MIDDLE EAST CRISIS DEEPENS

May 23, Cairo, Egypt Egypt has closed the Straits of Tiran to Israeli ships, shutting off Israel's only outlet to the Indian Ocean. The blockade comes after the withdrawal of United Nations' troops from Sinai at Egypt's request. This UN peace-keeping force has kept the Israelis and Egyptians apart for the past ten years. Egypt is threatening Israel by massing 100,000 troops and 1,000 tanks in Sinai, close to the Israeli border.

A column of Israeli soldiers on the march in Israel to confront Arab forces.

LIGHTNING STRIKE ON ARAB AIR POWER

June 6, Tel Aviv, Israel At breakfast time yesterday, Israeli aircraft appeared over Egypt's main airfields. From intelligence reports the Israelis knew that most Egyptian aircraft would be grounded at that time of day. Within hours, the Egyptian air force had been destroyed. In the afternoon, Israeli planes struck at airfields in Jordan, Syria, and Iraq. The result there was the same. By yesterday evening, the Arab air forces had ceased to exist. On the ground, Israeli armored columns have attacked and broken through Egyptian positions in Sinai.

EGYPT AND JORDAN ACCEPT CEASE-FIRE

June 7, Tel Aviv Israeli troops have reached the Suez Canal and now occupy the entire Sinai Peninsula. During the battle, hundreds of Egyptian tanks and vehicles jammed in the Mitla Pass were destroyed as they attempted to retreat westward. On the eastern front, the Israelis have driven the Jordanians out of East Jerusalem and from the West Bank area of Palestine. Israel, Egypt, and Jordan have accepted the cease-fire put forward by the United Nations. Fighting between them has ended. The war with Syria in the Golan Heights goes on. However, the end seems near.

MIDDLE EAST FIGHTING ENDS

June 10, Tel Aviv The Israelis have driven the Syrians from the Golan Heights and Syria has agreed to the UN cease-fire. Israel's victory is complete. In this Six-Day War, its armies have captured East Jerusalem, the West Bank, the Sinai Peninsula, and the Golan Heights. Israel has increased its territory size by more than 200 percent. The cost has been great, however, and over 100,000 lives are feared lost. The Israeli army leader, General Moshe Dayan, has been acclaimed a national hero. Yet long-term peace in the Middle East is as far off as ever. The Israelis may feel safer behind their new borders, but the Arabs say they will never rest until they have regained their lost lands and set up an Arab state of Palestine.

REAGAN IS CALIFORNIA GOVERNOR

Jan. 1, Sacramento, Cal. Ronald Reagan, a former movie actor, has been inaugurated governor of California. Reagan, a Republican, has never before run for public office. He defeated California's Democratic governor, Edmund G. (Pat) Brown, in November's election. Movie goers may remember Reagan from such films as *Kings Row* and *Bedtime for Bonzo*. He also hosted a television series.

ARMY COLONELS SEIZE GREECE

April 21, Athens A group of right-wing army officers, called the "junta" of colonels, today seized power from the democratic government. The junta is led by Colonel Georges Papadopoulos, in the name of the Greek king. The democratic leader, Georges Papandreou, is under arrest.

DE GAULLE SAYS "NON"

May 16, Paris Britain's latest application to join the European Common Market is certain to be turned down. President de Gaulle of France is against it. He maintains that the British are attached too closely to the Americans to be allowed into the European Community.

NIGERIA BREAKS UP

May 30, Enugu, Nigeria The Ibo people in eastern Nigeria have broken away from the rest of the country and set up an independent state they call Biafra. The Ibo leader Colonel Ojukwu accuses the other Nigerian peoples of deliberate attempts to wipe out the Ibos. A separate state is the Ibo's only chance of survival, he says.

WAR IN BIAFRA

July 31, Enugu Nigeria is now at war with the breakaway state of Biafra. The main fighting is in the north, as federal Nigerian troops try to advance toward the Biafran capital here in Enugu.

NO END TO VIETNAM WAR

Nov. 21, Saigon, South Vietnam American aircraft have made the heaviest raids of the war so far on North Vietnam. Apart from military damage, many civilians have been killed in the attacks. At home in the United States, opposition to the Vietnam War is growing. There are now over 450,000 Americans serving in Vietnam.

An anti-war demonstration is broken up by police.

WITH THE VIETCONG

Dec. 10, near Hanoi "Through the daylight hours nothing moves on the roads of North Vietnam, not a car nor a truck. It must look from the air as though the country had no wheeled transport at all. That, of course, is the idea, it is the roads and bridges that are being bombed; it is no longer safe after sunrise to be anywhere near either . . .

When the sun goes down everything starts to move . . . At dusk the roads become alive. The engines are started and the convoys grind away through the darkness behind the pinpoints of masked headlamps. There are miles of them, heavy Russian-built trucks, anti-aircraft batteries, all deeply buried under piles of branches and leaves . . . North Vietnam by day is abandoned; by night it thuds and grinds with movement. It is a fatiguing routine: working by day and moving by night."

(James Cameron, from *What a way to own the tribe*, Macmillan 1968)

NEWS IN BRIEF . . .

FIRST BLACK ON SUPREME COURT

Aug. 30, Washington, D.C. Thurgood Marshall, solicitor general of the United States, today became the first black on the Supreme Court. Nominated by President Lyndon Johnson, the Senate confirmed his nomination by a 69–11 vote. As chief legal officer for the National Association for the Advancement of Colored People (NAACP), he won 29 out of 32 cases before the Supreme Court. His best-known case overturned legal segregation of schools.

Justice Marshall and his family.

The first public showing of Concorde.

CONCORDE UNVEILED

Dec. 11, Toulouse, France The public has had its first glimpse of the Concorde. This morning test model 001, being built by the French at Toulouse, was rolled out onto the tarmac. The French and British aircraft industries are working together to develop and build the Concorde. It will be the world's first supersonic passenger aircraft and is a fine example of Anglo-French cooperation.

ASTRONAUTS DIE IN FIRE

Jan. 27, Cape Kennedy, Fla. Three American astronauts were killed today in the worst accident of the U.S. space program. A flash fire broke out aboard the spacecraft *Apollo 1* while it was still on the launching pad. Killed in the blaze were Virgil I. Grissom, Edward H. White, and Robert B. Chaffee. NASA officials believe that an electrical spark ignited the pure oxygen within the Apollo's cabin. The astronauts were trapped, unable to use the spacecraft's escape route because it was blocked by a gantry. The men were aboard the craft as part of the preparation for the actual launching, which was scheduled for February 21. The men were to remain in orbit for 14 days. This tragedy is a serious blow to the Apollo program and a great loss to the country.

Astronauts Grissom (left), White (center), and Chaffee shortly before their tragic deaths.

MAN GIVEN NEW HEART

Dec. 3, Cape Town, South Africa Surgeon Christiaan Barnard has carried out the first successful transplant of a human heart. The patient is doing well. According to Dr. Barnard, the operation was straightforward but he says that no one knows yet whether the patient's body will accept the new heart.

Dr. Christian Barnard, the South African surgeon

ELVIS MARRIES IN VEGAS

May 1, Las Vegas Elvis Presley, 32, the "king" of rock and roll, was married here today to Priscilla Beaulieu, 21. The bride and groom met in 1959 in Germany. The singer was serving in the Army. His bride was the daughter of an Air Force lieutenant colonel.

1968

AMERICA'S RACIAL VIOLENCE

SNIPER KILLS MARTIN LUTHER KING

April 4, Memphis, Tenn. The civil rights leader Dr. Martin Luther King, Jr., has been shot dead. He was talking to friends on their motel balcony when the bullet, fired from a distance, struck and killed him. The murderer escaped.

THOUSANDS MOURN MARTIN LUTHER KING

April 9, Atlanta Dr. Martin Luther King has had a hero's burial. Over 150,000 people crowded into Atlanta for his funeral. The coffin passed through the grieving multitude, lying on a plain wooden farm cart drawn by two mules. At the graveside, a recording of the dead man's last sermon was played as his own funeral oration.

Friends join hands at the funeral in Atlanta, Georgia, of Dr. Martin Luther King.

34

1968

AMERICA BURNS AFTER KING'S MURDER

April 11, Washington Martin Luther King's murder has stirred up widespread violence. Across America, mobs of angry blacks ran into the streets when they heard that the peace-loving leader had been shot. Over 100 cities felt the fury of the rioters. Here in the capital, tanks and armored cars came out to patrol the streets, and buildings were set ablaze within sight of the White House.

AFTER THE VIOLENCE

Dec. 17, Washington Martin Luther King did not die in vain. Thanks to him and to those he led, the laws that denied rights to black Americans have been swept away. But racial prejudice in America is far from over, and racial violence will return. The struggle that Martin Luther King, Jr., led for full equality for all Americans must go on.

BOBBY KENNEDY SHOT DEAD

June 6, Los Angeles A 20-hour fight to save the life of Senator Robert Kennedy has failed. Kennedy was campaigning here for the Democratic presidential nomination when he was shot at point-blank range. The killer is a Jordanian Arab. He shouted "I did it for my country!" as Kennedy fell, mortally wounded. It is believed that Kennedy's support for Israel made him a target for supporters of the Palestinian cause in the Middle East.

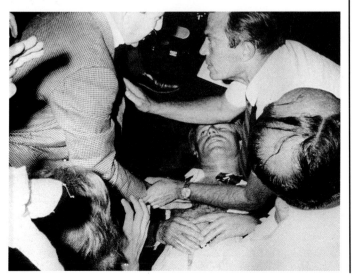

REBELS LOSING NIGERIAN WAR

May 8, Lagos, Nigeria Nigerian troops have captured Port Harcourt and now occupy most of the main centers of population in the breakaway state of Biafra. However, the Biafran rebels still control large areas around the cities. They are determined to continue to fight even though they can have no hope of winning the war.

A Biafran soldier awaits advancing Nigerian forces.

NIXON TO BE NEXT PRESIDENT

Nov. 6, Washington The Republican candidate Richard Nixon has been elected President of the United States. This was Nixon's second attempt to enter the White House. In the election eight years ago he was narrowly defeated by John F. Kennedy. The new President inherits immense problems. Among them are the global Cold War between capitalism and communism, the war in Vietnam, and continuing violence in our towns and cities.

x

THE PRAGUE SPRING

THE CZECHS EDGE TOWARD FREEDOM

March 13, Prague Czechoslovakia has been in the grip of the Soviet Union since 1945 when World War II ended. Since then, the Czechs have endured the same harsh laws as the people of the other Communist countries of Eastern Europe. But now the government of Alexander Dubcek has ended censorship. From today, newspapers in Czechoslovakia are free to print the news as they see it. Dubcek came to power in January. Thanks to his reforms this "Prague Spring," there is already more liberty in Czechoslovakia than in any other country on the Soviet side of the Iron Curtain.

Alexander Dubcek surrounded by his supporters.

SOVIET TANKS ROLL INTO PRAGUE TO CRUSH CZECH LIBERTY

Aug. 22, Prague Soviet troops and tanks occupy Prague. Alexander Dubcek and his senior ministers have been arrested. Communist party officials who opposed the Dubcek reforms have replaced them and Czechoslovakia is back under Soviet control. The Czech people are in despair, for they are powerless to resist the Russian invasion. Soviet newspapers claim that the Czechs are grateful to the Russian troops for putting an end to the Dubcek regime.

Soviet tanks entering Prague on the first day of the invasion of Czechoslovakia.

NEWS IN BRIEF . . .

RUSSIAN SPACEMAN KILLED

March 27, Moscow Yuri Gagarin, the first man into space, is dead. He was killed today when the aircraft he was piloting crashed, 31 miles (50 km) from Moscow.

ZEPPELIN OVER AMERICA

Dec. 15, New York Britain has provided the biggest new rock music act of the year in this country. Led Zeppelin, a group put together by guitarist Jimmy Page, has stunned America with its amazingly powerful sound. Another group, Cream, isn't far behind. The local reply to the British invasion hasn't been slow in coming. Blue Cheer, Iron Butterfly, and Spirit led the bands in America's charts.

ASTRONAUTS CIRCLE THE MOON

Dec. 27, Cape Kennedy, Fla. A space-craft carrying three astronauts splashed down into the Pacific today after a six-day mission that took it ten times around the moon. U.S. space officials are delighted with the success of this mission. Their next target is the moon itself.

Black Olympic athletes give the black power salute.

BLACK POWER AT MEXICO OLYMPICS

Oct. 27, Mexico City Politics rather than athletics have been the main feature of these games. Two black American athletes, standing on the victors' rostrum, raised a black-gloved fist in a defiant black power salute under the American national flag while the American national anthem was being played. Their protest was watched by millions of television viewers worldwide. The two runners were making a personal sacrifice; they were later expelled from the American Olympic team and sent home.

1969

MEN ON THE MOON
THE MOON FLIGHT BEGINS

July 16, Kennedy Space Center, Fla. At 9:32 this morning, *Apollo 11* took off for the moon. Three thousand reporters were at the site, and a million sightseers jammed the roads around the Kennedy Space Center. They cheered and prayed as the 364-foot-high (111 m-) Saturn rocket rose from its launch pad and headed up into the sky over the Atlantic. Around the world, 600 million television viewers watched the liftoff. The three astronauts, Neil Armstrong, "Buzz" Aldrin, and Michael Collins, are now on course for a moon landing four days from now. The world watches and waits.

"WE HAVE NO COMPLAINTS"

July 19, Houston Space Center Everything has gone according to plan. The Saturn rocket boosted the command module *Columbia* and the lunar module *Eagle* to a speed of 24,800 mph (40,000 kph) before falling away and burning up in the earth's atmosphere. The crew are pleased with the flight so far. "It was beautiful. We have no complaints," said Neil Armstrong, the *Apollo 11* commander, during one of yesterday's television transmissions from *Columbia* as it hurtled on its path toward its goal—the moon.

Apollo 11 lifts off at Kennedy Space Center. Crew members are Neil Armstrong, Michael Collins, and Edwin "Buzz" Aldrin. Armstrong and Aldrin are due to land on the moon on July 20.

The lunar module approaches the surface of the moon.

THE EAGLE HAS LANDED | SAFELY BACK TO EARTH

July 21, Houston Space Center Cameras on board the mooncraft beamed back to earth pictures of the final moments of *Eagle's* descent to the dusty surface of the moon. At 3:17 p.m. Houston time yesterday, a sigh of relief went up around the world as Neil Armstrong guided the *Eagle* the last few yards to a safe landing. A minute later he made his historic report back to earth, "The *Eagle* has landed." Four hours later, Armstrong and Aldrin struggled into their bulky space suits and prepared to step out onto the moon.

July 24, *USS Hornet*, Pacific Ocean The *Columbia* splashed down into the Pacific earlier today. President Nixon is here on board the aircraft carrier *Hornet* to welcome the returned astronauts. But no one, not even the President of the United States, is allowed to shake their hands or meet them face to face. The astronauts are wearing special clothing and are living in a sealed container. They will stay there until tests prove that they did not pick up some deadly infection during their visit to the moon.

Edwin "Buzz" Aldrin walks on the moon. Neil Armstrong is reflected in his helmet.

A VIEW FROM THE MOON

July 21, The moon "The sky is black, you know . . . It's a peculiar thing, but the surface looked very warm and inviting."

Neil Armstrong

"Still don't know exactly what color to describe this other than greyish-cocoa color. It appears to be covering most of the lighter part of my boot . . . very fine particles . . ."

Edwin Aldrin

(From *First on the Moon*, Farmer and Hamblin, Michael Joseph 1970)

MOON PROGRAM QUESTIONED

Dec. 31, Washington The second moon shot last month was another technical triumph. The craft managed to land within 3,300 feet (1,000 m) of an unmanned moon probe sent up in 1967. The astronauts collected 75 pounds (34 kg) of rock and set up several experiments. Amazingly clear pictures of the moon were beamed back to TV sets on earth. But the future of the moon program is uncertain. A fifth of the world's population watched the first moon landing but since then it seems that nobody is interested in space any more. Many scientists doubt that the benefits to science of the moon landings are worth the colossal cost.

NEWS IN BRIEF . . .

CZECHOSLOVAKIA MOURNS A MARTYR

Jan. 25, Prague On January 19, Jan Palach, a 21-year-old student, burned himself to death in Prague's Wenceslas Square. His suicide was a protest against the Soviet occupation of his country. When he was buried today, hundreds of thousands of Czechs lined the streets of Prague to pay tribute to his sacrifice.

Jan Palach's grave in Prague.

NEW LEADER FOR PALESTINE GUERRILLAS
Feb. 3, Cairo The new head of the Palestine Liberation Organization is to be Yasser Arafat. Arafat is a Palestinian; he was born in Jerusalem in 1929. In 1963 he founded the Al Fatah movement to win back Palestine from the Israelis.

Yasser Arafat.

EISENHOWER DEAD AT 78
March 28, Washington Dwight D. Eisenhower died here today. Eisenhower, a former five-star general, led the Allies to victory in World War II. He was elected President in 1952, and reelected in 1956. President Nixon said Eisenhower "held a unique place in America's history."

N.Y. METS WIN WORLD SERIES
Oct. 16, New York The New York Mets finally won a World Series. The much-mocked team beat the Baltimore Orioles in the fourth game of the Series. The whole city celebrated.

THE MAXI LOOK
Oct. 21, Paris The sixties will go down in fashion history as the decade of the miniskirt. But now the mini is dead. There was not a knee to be seen at the fashion shows here this autumn. The new "maxi" skirt ends just above the ankle and the audience loved it. It is worn with boots and an ankle-length coat.

PEOPLE OF THE SIXTIES

John Fitzgerald Kennedy 1917–1963

After winning medals for bravery in World War II, John Kennedy entered politics. In 1960 he was elected President of the United States. Aged 43, he was the youngest person and the first Roman Catholic to hold the office. He won the admiration and gratitude of the free world for his handling of the 1962 Cuban missile crisis and for his stand against the Soviet Union. Kennedy was assassinated in Dallas in 1963.

Martin Luther King, Jr. 1929–1968

Dr. King was a leading religious and civil rights campaigner in the United States. A Baptist minister like his father, Dr. King became a leader of America's black people in their struggle to win equal rights with the whites. A champion of nonviolence, he was awarded the Kennedy Peace Prize and, in 1964, the Nobel Peace Prize. He was murdered by a white racist in 1968. His memory inspires people throughout the world.

Lyndon Baines Johnson 1908–1973

Texan Democrat Lyndon Johnson was Senate Majority Leader during the 1950s. He became John F. Kennedy's Vice-President, and when Kennedy was assassinated in 1963, Johnson became President. He was elected for a full term in 1964. Johnson was in power when laws were passed that improved the position of blacks. The economy also improved. However, he was blamed for the failure of the U.S. to win the Vietnam War, and he gave up politics in 1968.

Nikita Sergeyevich Khrushchev 1894–1971

Nikita Khrushchev was born near Kursk in Russia, and joined the Communist party in 1918. He became head of the Communist Soviet Union shortly after the death of Stalin. His attempt to set up nuclear missiles in Cuba almost led to war with the United States. After the crisis was over he adopted a more friendly approach toward the Western powers. His softer policies won him many powerful enemies in the Soviet Union and they forced him out of office in 1964.

Muhammad Ali, boxer 1942–

Ali began his career as Cassius Clay, but changed his name to Muhammad Ali when he converted to the Black Muslim faith. In 1964 he beat Sonny Liston to become World Heavyweight Champion. Ali became a hero to sports fans and black people everywhere. He supported the black rights movement and opposed the war in Vietnam. When he refused to fight in the war he was arrested and stripped of his title. He returned to the ring and regained the title in 1974, and again in 1978. In 1975, he published an autobiography called *The Greatest: My Own Story*.

Indira Gandhi 1917–1984

Indira Gandhi was the daughter of Jawaharlal Nehru, the first prime minister of India after independence. She joined her father's Congress party and worked with him in the struggle to free India from British rule. She was elected to Parliament and in 1959 became president of the Congress party. In 1964, after her father died, she entered the Cabinet as minister of information. Two years later she became India's third prime minister and went on to serve as India's prime minister four times. In 1984 she was assassinated by her Sikh bodyguard. Indira Gandhi's son, Rajiv, then became prime minister.

Alexander Dubcek 1921–

In 1968, after a long period of general economic decline, food shortages, and other problems in Czechoslovakia, Alexander Dubcek was made head of the Communist government. When he lifted censorship and began to introduce freedoms of other kinds in Czechoslovakia, Soviet troops invaded the country and put an end to his reforms. Dubcek was disgraced and forced out of politics. He returned to public life and was honored as a pioneer of Czech freedom when the Communist government was overthrown in 1989.

Billie Jean King 1943–

Billie Jean King was born Billie Jean Moffitt in California. At school she was good at all games but took up tennis when she was given an eight-dollar tennis racket. In her long career, Billie Jean King won over 50 championships including 20 at Wimbledon. When she became a top-ranking player in the sixties, men players were paid more than twice as much as women. Mrs. King campaigned hard for equal pay for women. Thanks to her efforts, men and women players are now treated equally.

American Firsts

1960   First televised debates between presidential
candidates took place.
First aerial recovery of satellites achieved.
American flag orbits the earth, in
Discoverer XIII.
Electronic wristwatches go on sale, New York.

1961   Presidential news conference televised live.
First skyjack of a commercial American airplane
took place.
Alan B. Shepard is first American astronaut
launched into space.
Roger Maris is first major-league baseball player
to hit more than 60 home runs in a season.

1962   First Native American graduated from Air Force
Academy: Leo Johnson.
A telephone hotline from the White House to the
Russian Kremlin is set up.
First black woman judge takes office:
E.S. Sampson, Chicago.

1963   A measles vaccine was developed by a virologist
team led by John F. Enders.
Push-button telephones go into use, Penn.
Marian Anderson is first black woman to be
awarded the Medal of Freedom.

1964   First freeze-dried coffee marketed.
An American spacecraft reaches the moon.
Sidney Poitier is the first black to win a best-
actor Oscar.
Margaret Chase Smith is first woman to
campaign for presidential nomination for a
major party.
Presidential election results tallied electronically.

1965   L.E. Lockwood of Arizona, is first female chief
justice named to a state supreme court.
First all-news radio station begins broadcasting.
First federal health insurance plan (Medicare)
put into effect.

1966 Neil Armstrong is first American civilian to orbit the earth.
First photograph of the earth from the moon is taken.

1967 *The New York Times* published the first large-type newspaper.
First state legislation legalizing abortion was signed, Colorado.
First black Supreme Court justice, Thurgood Marshall, was sworn in.

1968 Federal law authorizing observance of major holidays on Mondays was enacted.
Shirley Chisholm, New York, was first black woman elected to House of Representatives.

1969 Astronauts transfer from one spacecraft to another.
The first telephone call was made from the earth to the moon.

New words and expressions

New words and expressions are constantly being added to the English language. Many of those that first appeared in the sixties arose from rock music, space travel, the civil rights movement, computers, and war.

acid rock	hard rock
affirmative action	mainframe
banana seat	meltdown
Black Panther	microchip
black power	mind-blowing
catch-22	Peace Corps
counterculture	peace sign
counter intelligence	pop art
disaster area	rip-off
fast-food	security blanket
flaky	sit com
flower children	space shuttle
freedom rider	space walk
green card	take-out food
groupie	uptight
hang-up	wheeler-dealer

How many of these words and expressions do we still use today? Do you know what they all mean?

Glossary

apartheid: the policy of the South African Nationalist party, of keeping white people apart from people of other races and giving them many privileges.

Black Muslims: a group of mostly black persons who profess the Islamic faith.

black power: in the 1960s the black peoples of America grouped themselves together to fight for equality with the whites. They called their combined strength "black power."

civil rights: the rights that people have to the same treatment and opportunities, no matter what their race, religion, or sex may be.

cold war: hostility between what was the USSR and the United States that stopped short of war.

colony: a territory governed and controlled by people from another country.

contraception (contraceptive): any method of preventing pregnancy; birth control.

convoy: a protective escort for ships sailing during periods of war or warlike activity.

fallout: pieces of radioactive material produced by a nuclear explosion.

federal marshal: an officer apointed by the government to keep law and order.

guerrilla: someone who fights as part of an irregular army, not part of the official forces of the state; (from a Spanish word meaning "little war").

holocaust: complete destruction or mass slaughter.

Indochina: in Southeast Asia, the countries of Laos, Cambodia, and Vietnam.

orbit: the path of one body as it revolves around another. The earth orbits the sun; spacecraft make orbits around the earth.

Palestine: the Arab name for Israel, a country at the eastern end of the Mediterranean.

pass laws: in South Africa the laws that compelled nonwhite people to carry passes to enable them to travel about in their own country. Pass laws were one of the main features of apartheid.

racist: anyone who is prejudiced or who practices discrimination based solely on the belief that one race of people is superior to another.

regime: a system or method of government e.g. a fascist regime.

sabotage: deliberate damage done to something such as a piece of machinery to stop it working.

summit: a meeting between the top leaders of nations, rather than lower level officials.

supersonic: something, usually aircraft, that is able to move faster than the speed of sound in air.

townships: areas on the outskirts of South African towns where most nonwhite people have been obliged to live. Sharpeville was a township near Vereeniging south of Johannesburg.

Further Reading

Anderson, Catherine C. *John F. Kennedy.* Lerner, 1991

Cairns, Trevor. *Twentieth Century.* Lerner, 1984

Carey, Helen and Greenberg, Judith. *How to Read a Newspaper.* Watts, 1983

——*How to Use Primary Sources.* Watts, 1983

Connickie, Yvonne. *The Nineteen Sixties.* Facts on File

Crocker, Chris. *Great American Astronauts.* Watts, 1988

Devaney, John. *Lyndon Baines Johnson, President.* Walker & Co., 1986

Grey, Edward. *The Sixties.* "Decades" series. Raintree Steck-Vaughn, 1990

Hess, Debra. *Thurgood Marshall: The Fight for Equal Justice.* Silver Burdett Pr., 1990

Kosof, Anna. *The Civil Rights Movement and Its Legacy.* Watts, 1989

Loewen, L. *The Beatles.* Rourke Corp., 1989

Primlott, John. *The Cold War.* Watts, 1987

——Middle East: *A Background to the Conflicts.* Watts, 1991

Rowland, Delta. *Martin Luther King, Jr. The Dream of Peaceful Revolution.* Silver Burdett Pr., 1990

Index

Aberfan 29
Aldrin, Edwin "Buzz" 38, 40
Al Fatah 30, 41
Algeria 9, 10
Ali, Muhammad (Cassius Clay) 22, 43
Arabs 21, 30, 31
Arafat, Yasser 41
Armstrong, Neil 38, 40, 41
Australia 28

Beatles 19
Berlin Wall 11
Biafra 31, 35
black power 37
Brezhnev 21

Castro, Fidel 13
Chichester, Francis 28
China 20, 23, 27
Churchill, Sir Winston 26
Communists 11, 20, 36
Concorde 33
Congo 10
Coventry Cathedral 16
Cuba 13, 14, 15
Cyprus 22
Czechoslovakia 36, 41

De Gaulle, Charles 10, 31
Dubcek, Alexander 36, 43

Egypt 30, 31
Eichmann, Adolf 13
Eisenhower, Dwight D. 8, 41
European Common Market 31

Gagarin, Yuri 12, 37
Gandhi, Indira 28, 43
Germany, East 11
Glenn, John 16
Golan Heights 31
Greeks 22, 31

Ibos 31
India 23, 28
Iraq 13, 31
Israel 13, 30, 31

Johnson, Lyndon B. 17, 18, 21, 25, 26, 42
Jordan 31

Kennedy, John F. 9, 13, 14, 17, 18, 35, 42
Kennedy, Robert 35
Khrushchev, Nikita 8, 21, 42
King, Billie Jean 43
King, Martin Luther 18, 23, 25, 34, 35, 42
Kosygin, Alexei 21
Kuwait 13

Led Zeppelin 37
Lumumba, Patrice 10

Makarios, Archbishop 22
Malcolm X 26
Mandela, Nelson 15, 23
Mao Tse-tung 27
March on Washington 18
Marshall, Thurgood 32
maxi skirt 41
Middle East 30, 31, 35
miniskirt 26
Mobutu, Joseph 10
Monroe, Marilyn 16
moon mission 37, 38, 39, 40, 41

Nehru, Jawaharlal 28
Nigeria 10, 31, 35
Nixon, Richard M. 9, 16, 35, 40

Ojukwu, Odumegwu 31
Olympic Games 23, 37
Oswald, Lee Harvey 17, 18

Palach, Jan 41
Palestine 21, 31
Palestine Liberation Organization 21, 41
Peace Corps 13
Pope John XXIII 19
Powers, Gary 8
Presley, Elvis 33
Profumo, John 19

Quant, Mary 26

Reagan, Ronald 31
Red Guards 27
Ruby, Jack 18

Sharpeville 9
South Africa 9, 10, 15, 23, 29
Soviet Union (Russia) 8, 10, 12, 13, 14, 20, 21, 36
Syria 30, 31

Tonkin, Gulf of 21
Turks 22

United Kingdom (Britain) 16, 19, 26, 28
United Nations Organization 30, 31
United States of America 8, 9, 14, 15, 16, 17, 20, 21, 24, 26, 32, 34, 35, 37, 38

Verwoerd, Hendrik 10, 29
Vietnam 13, 20, 21, 28, 32

Warhol, Andy 16

©Copyright 1992 Evans Brothers Limited

47